SCATALOG
A Kid's Field Guide to Animal Poop

HOW TO TRACK
A TURKEY

Norman D. Graubart

"BECAUSE EVERYBODY POOPS"

WINDMILL
BOOKS
New York

Published in 2015 by Windmill Books, an Imprint of Rosen Publishing
29 East 21st Street, New York, NY 10010

First Edition

Editor: Katie Kawa
Book Design: Michael J. Flynn

Photo Credits: Cover (turkey), p. 11 Bruce MacQueen/Shutterstock.com; cover (leaves) Franck Boston/Shutterstock.com; cover, p. 17 (gobbler poop) Jennifer Schlick/Flickr; back cover, pp. 1, 3–8, 10–12, 14–20, 22–24 (turkey feathers) nbiebach/Shutterstock.com; p. 4 Jeff Banke/Shutterstock.com; pp. 5, 7, 11, 15, 17, 19 (turkey tracks) ntnt/Shutterstock.com; pp. 5, 17 (hen poop) by Michael Flynn; p. 6 Tim Laman/National Geographic/Getty Images; p. 7 pavalena/Shutterstock.com; p. 8 Steve & Dave Maslowski/Photo Researchers/Getty Images; pp. 9, 21 Tom Reichner/Shutterstock.com; p. 10 © iStockphoto/HKPNC; p. 12 NeonLight/Shutterstock.com; p. 13 Leonard Lee Rue III/Photo Researchers/Getty Images; p. 14 © iStockphoto/driftlessstudio; p. 15 Ksanawo/Shutterstock.com; p. 16 © iStockphoto/Jens_Lambert_Photography; p. 18 Sharon Day/Shutterstock.com; p. 19 S.J. Krasemann/Photolibrary/Getty Images; p. 20 Stephanie Frey/Shutterstock.com; p. 22 Mike Grandmaison/All Canada Photos/Getty Images.

Library of Congress Cataloging-in-Publication Data

Graubart, Norman D., author.
 How to track a turkey / Norman D. Graubart.
     pages cm. — (Scatalog : a kid's field guide to animal poop)
 Includes index.
 ISBN 978-1-4777-5419-1 (pbk.)
 ISBN 978-1-4777-5420-7 (6 pack)
 ISBN 978-1-4777-5414-6 (library binding)
 1. Wild turkey—Juvenile literature. 2. Animal droppings—Juvenile literature. 3. Animal tracks—Juvenile literature. 4. Tracking and trailing—Juvenile literature. [1. Turkeys.] I. Title.
 QL696.G27G73 2015
 598.6'45—dc23
                              2014028302

Manufactured in the United States of America

CPSIA Compliance Information: Batch # CW15WM: For Further Information contact Rosen Publishing, New York, New York at 1-800-237-9932

CONTENTS

TRACKING TURKEYS

The turkey has been a popular game bird in the United States since the country's earliest days. Many Americans eat turkey on Thanksgiving, and children often draw pictures of turkeys for this holiday, too.

Turkeys lived in North America long before the United States was its own country.

seed

Turkey poop can tell trackers a lot about turkeys. For example, the turkey that left this behind ate a lot of seeds!

Americans have been hunting turkeys for hundreds of years. Turkeys are hunted for sport and also for their meat. To find turkeys, hunters need to track them. They can track turkeys by doing many things, including looking for turkey footprints and listening for the sounds they make. Another way hunters track turkeys is by looking for their poop!

WHERE TURKEYS LIVE

Turkeys are common in North America. They live mostly in the eastern and midwestern parts of the United States. They can also be found in Mexico. Although turkeys are found all over North America, they like to live in a certain kind of **habitat**.

Trackers sometimes find turkey feathers near trees where turkeys are roosting.

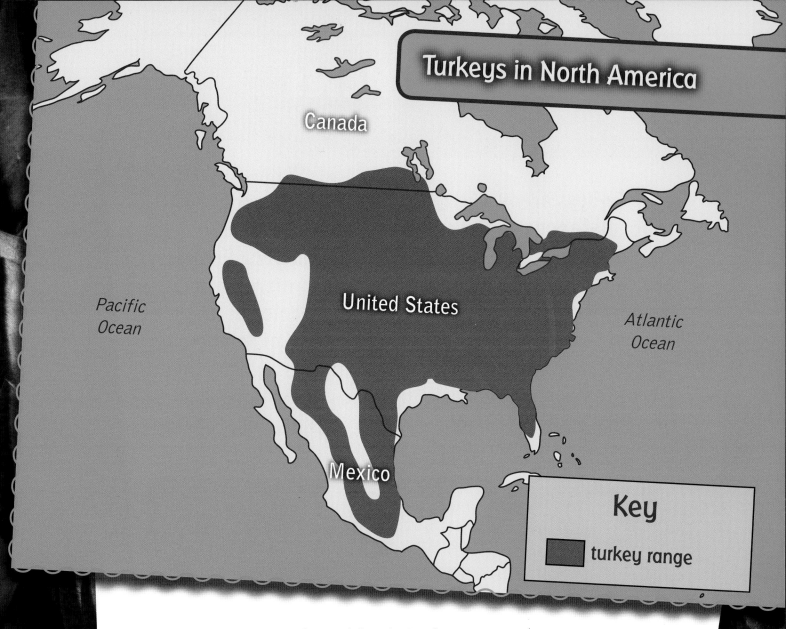

Turkeys in North America

Canada

Pacific
Ocean

United States

Atlantic
Ocean

Mexico

Key

turkey range

Turkeys are found both in forests and open areas, such as meadows. Forests give turkeys places to find food and hide from predators. Turkeys often roost, or rest in trees, at night. Open spaces give turkeys other places to eat, as well as places to **mate**.

GOBBLERS AND HENS

Turkeys aren't like most birds. They can only fly short **distances** because of how big their body is.

Male turkeys are called toms or gobblers. Females are called hens. Gobblers are bigger and more colorful than hens. A gobbler's head can change color during the mating season. It also has a long "beard" of feathers on its chest and **spurs** on the back of its legs. It has a big fan of feathers on its back, too. Hens are smaller and don't have a fan of feathers. Most hens also don't have a beard or spurs.

> Hens are less colorful than gobblers because they need to blend in with their surroundings when they're sitting on their nest.

Gobblers got their name because the sound they make is called a gobble.

LIFE IN A FLOCK

Turkeys live in small groups called rafters. Hens live with other hens, and gobblers live with gobblers. The oldest hens and gobblers are commonly the leaders of their group.

The group of female turkeys that a male turkey mates with is called a harem.

When gobblers strut, they spread out their wing feathers until they touch the ground. This leaves marks behind called wingtip marks, which can be used to track turkeys.

During mating season, a gobbler will find a group of females to mate with. This happens in the first few weeks of spring. Gobblers spread out their colorful feathers to **attract** hens. This is called strutting. Turkeys aren't the only animals that strut. You may have seen a peacock fan out its feathers at the zoo!

A TURKEY'S LIFE CYCLE

After turkeys mate, hens lay 8 to 15 spotted eggs. The hens watch over their eggs until the baby turkeys are ready to come out. Then, the baby turkeys join the group of hens and learn to find food. These groups can become very large!

Wild turkeys commonly live to be three or four years old. Turkeys are **prey** for many North American predators, including coyotes, foxes, raccoons, and owls. People are turkey predators, too. Hunters have to track turkeys in order to find them.

Hens **protect** their babies from predators that want to eat them. Gobblers don't stay with the babies.

Predators, such as the red fox, hunt turkeys and steal turkey eggs out of their nests!

THE DIGESTIVE SYSTEM

Turkeys find food by foraging, which means looking around for things to eat. Even though turkeys can fly, they commonly forage by walking around and looking on or near the ground. They look for bugs, nuts, seeds, and even salamanders. The food they eat depends on the time of year, because different types of food are on the ground at different times.

The waste left over after a turkey's body breaks down food comes out of the turkey as poop.

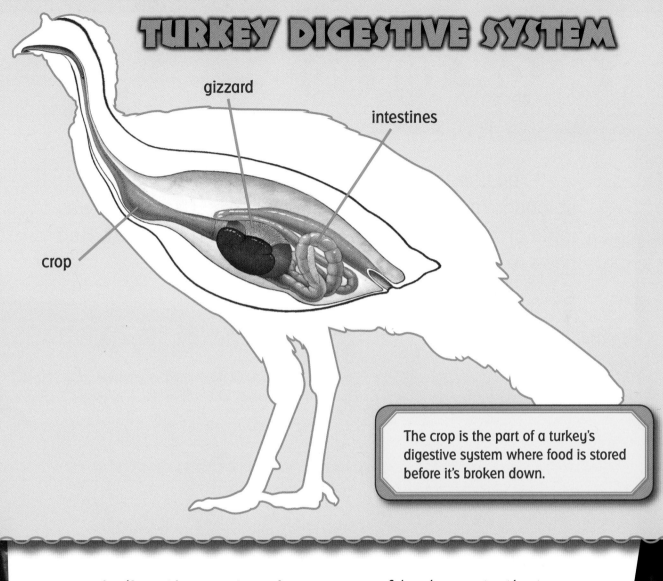

TURKEY DIGESTIVE SYSTEM

gizzard

intestines

crop

The crop is the part of a turkey's digestive system where food is stored before it's broken down.

A digestive system is a group of body parts that breaks down food into stuff a body can use. A turkey's digestive system has many parts. Like all birds, turkeys have a gizzard, which is a special stomach part that grinds up the food a turkey eats.

FOLLOW THE POOP!

You can learn a lot about a turkey by looking at its poop. You can tell whether the turkey that left it was male or female. Gobbler poop is long and j-shaped. Hen poop is smaller and looks like popcorn.

It's easy to tell if a turkey is a gobbler or a hen. You can even tell by looking at its poop!

GOBBLER POOP AND HEN POOP

GOBBLER		HEN
longer than hen poop	SIZE	smaller than gobbler poop
j-shaped	SHAPE	popcorn-shaped
many pieces (gobblers poop while they move)	AMOUNT	one small pile

Dark, wet turkey poop is fresh. The turkey that left it might still be nearby. Older poop is light brown or white and dry. The turkey that left it may not be in the area anymore. Hunters and other people who track turkeys can find places where turkeys roost by looking for poop at the base of trees.

You also can track turkeys by looking for their footprints. Turkey tracks show three long, thin toes. Tracks left by a gobbler show a middle toe that's longer than the other two toes. Turkeys are heavy animals, so their tracks can be deep and easy to find. Bigger tracks mean bigger turkeys!

Gobbler tracks are larger than hen tracks.

long middle toe

4.5 inches (11 cm)

three toes

A dust bowl is a sign that a turkey was dusting itself in the area and may return to that spot to do it again.

You may also find a **shallow** pit in a dusty area. This is a dust bowl. Dust bowls are made when turkeys roll around in dust to get rid of little bugs that bother them. Turkeys also leave V-shaped scratch marks on the ground as they look for food.

HUNTING TURKEYS

Hunters find turkeys using other methods, too. These methods include turkey calls, which **imitate** the sounds turkeys make. You can buy a turkey call at a hunting store, or you can try making a turkey call with your own voice.

There are laws to follow when hunting turkeys. Make sure you have an adult hunter with you who knows the state's hunting laws. It can be illegal to hunt turkeys in the wrong place or at the wrong time of year. Hunting laws create a balance between having too many turkeys and not enough of them.

If you see signs that a turkey was in an area, such as tracks or poop, you could use a turkey call to find the bird. The turkey will answer your call with its own gobble.

It's important to follow hunting laws because they protect both the turkeys and the people who hunt them. The number of turkeys you can kill in a day or season is called the bag limit.

A HEALTHY BALANCE

In the early twentieth century, turkeys were hunted in such large numbers in North America that they almost disappeared completely. Since that time, people who care about animal populations have helped pass laws that protect wild turkeys.

Hunters aren't the only people who track turkeys. Scientists track these birds to learn more about them. Now that there's a healthy balance between hunting and protection, there will be wild turkeys all over North America for years to come. You might even be able to track a wild turkey—with help from an adult—in your own backyard!

GLOSSARY

attract (uh-TRAKT) To cause to come close.

distance (DIHS-tuhns) The space between two points.

habitat (HAA-buh-tat) The natural home for plants, animals, and other living things.

imitate (IH-muh-tayt) To copy.

mate (MAYT) To come together to make babies.

prey (PRAY) An animal hunted by other animals for food.

protect (pruh-TEHKT) To keep safe.

shallow (SHAA-loh) Not deep.

spur (SPUHR) A sharp spine on the leg of a bird.

INDEX

WEBSITES

For web resources related to the subject of this book, go to:
www.windmillbooks.com/weblinks and select this book's title.

24